THE CLEAR AND PRESENT TRUTH OF THE

DAILY SACRIFICE

Rapid Movements Publishing
Hampton, GA 30228

Printed in the United States of America

Published by Rapid Movements Publishing
Hampton, GA 30228

Other books by Tory St.Cyr may be purchased at
www.clearandpresenttruth.com

The author assumes full responsibility for the accuracy of all facts and quotations, as cited in this book.

ISBN: 978-1-7366073-0-5

This book is dedicated to all the early Seventh-day Adventist pioneers who studied the prophecies of Daniel and Revelation. Thank you for the foundation of prophetic excellence you helped instill in this church.

Contents

Preface

If you are reading this book, I believe you fall into one of three categories:

1) You have already studied the Daily Sacrifice and have an understanding of this subject based on that study. However, you are reading this book simply because you are curious to find out if this book's interpretation matches your own.
2) You have heard of The Daily Sacrifice but have never understood what it means. You are reading this book because you want to gain an understanding of this subject.
3) You have never heard of the Daily Sacrifice and possibly have little interest in understanding what it means. In fact, you aren't exactly sure how this book ended up in your hands.

If you are in the first category, I hope this book will give you a new perspective regarding the Daily Sacrifice.

If you are in the second category, understand that there are other believers who, like you, are vaguely acquainted with this subject. However, I honestly believe you will find the information written in this book to be of utmost interest to you.

If you are in the third category, I pray that you continue reading this book. I believe the Lord led you here for a reason; and if God led you here, then there is something in this book that He wants you to read.

Regardless of what category you are part of, God has a message for His Church in these last days, and I hope and pray that you are blessed by it.

Chapter 1

An Introduction To The Daily Sacrifice

The Daily - " *Tâmîyd,*" continuance (as indefinite extension); constant (or adverbially, constantly); elliptically the regular (daily) sacrifice:—alway(-s), continual (employment, -ly), daily, (n-)ever(-more), perpetual.[1]

Since my early twenties, I have been drawn to the prophecies of Daniel and Revelation. This attraction to prophecy was set in motion during my early adolescent years. As a young child, I can still remember my Dad pleading with my older siblings and me in an attempt to ~~scare~~ teach us what was coming upon this world in the last days of earth's history. Our family worships often consisted of words

[1] "H8548 - tamiyd - Strong's Hebrew Lexicon (KJV)." Blue Letter Bible. Accessed 15 Aug, 2020. https://www.blueletterbible.org//lang/lexicon/lexicon.cfm?Strongs=H8548&t=KJV

like *persecution*, *the mark of the beast*, *the seven last plagues*, and many other familiar phrases found in the pages of prophetic writ. However, there was one phrase that was never mentioned during family worship. As you can see, this phrase is also found on the front cover of this book, which unfortunately nullifies any attempt to add suspense before revealing it to you. Yes, you "guessed" it. The phrase is *The Daily Sacrifice*.

The Daily Sacrifice may sound a little anti-climactic, but I want to assure you that this phrase is far from that. As a matter of fact, this particular phrase is one of the most important yet misunderstood phrases in all the Book of Daniel.

Honestly, it wasn't until recently that I even gave a second look to the Daily Sacrifice. In my earlier years, I had the mindset that the Daily Sacrifice was literally what the Bible called it—a sacrifice that took place on a daily basis. Scripture confirms that certain sacrifices did occur on a day-by-day basis. Notice what the Bible says in Exodus 29:38:

> "Now this is that which thou shalt offer upon the altar; two lambs of the first year day by day continually."

I associated these day-to-day sacrifices with the Daily Sacrifice found in the Book of Daniel. However, it wasn't until I began writing *The Clear and*

Present Truth of Daniel 11 (Was that a shameless plug?) that I realized the Book of Daniel makes a total of five references to the Daily Sacrifice. Studying all five of these references made me realize that my understanding of the Daily Sacrifice did not add up. Before I detail the reasons, let me provide all five references to you in their entirety:

> "Yea, he magnified *himself* even to the prince of the host, and by him **the daily *sacrifice*** was taken away, and the place of his sanctuary was cast down." Daniel 8:11

> "And an host was given *him* against **the daily *sacrifice*** by reason of transgression, and it cast down the truth to the ground; and it practised, and prospered." Daniel 8:12

> "Then I heard one saint speaking, and another saint said unto that certain *saint* which spake, How long *shall* be the vision *concerning* **the daily *sacrifice***, and the transgression of desolation, to give both the sanctuary and the host to be trodden under foot?" Daniel 8:13

> "And arms shall stand on his part, and they shall pollute the sanctuary of strength, and shall take away **the daily *sacrifice***, and they shall place the abomination that maketh desolate." Daniel 11:31

> "And from the time *that* **the daily *sacrifice*** shall be taken away, and the abomination that maketh desolate set up, *there shall be* a thousand two hundred and ninety days." Daniel 12:11

As I studied these five verses, I realized my current understanding of the Daily Sacrifice left too many questions unanswered. Questions like—Who was Daniel referring to when he said, "*by him the daily sacrifice was taken away*"? When would this sacrifice be taken away? Why was the sacrifice taken away? And last but not least—How is this relevant for me today? With no clear answers to these questions, I began to wonder if the Daily Sacrifice referred to something other than the Jewish sacrificial system.

I want you to understand that I am not an individual who believes in something just because a Pastor or Bible scholar said it. Some might even say the "Bible scholars" and "Pastor's" during the time of Jesus' earthy ministry all had misinterpreted the scriptures. It was mostly laypeople who were given an understanding of things the scholars misunderstood. But I digress. Once I realized that I had no idea what the Daily Sacrifice was, I decided that I would dedicate most of my study time to understanding what those two words really meant.

Looking in the Bible for any other references to the Daily Sacrifice, I clearly saw that this phrase was exclusively attributed to the prophet Daniel by the King James translation. However, that hardly got me closer to understanding exactly what the phrase meant. As a matter of fact, an argument can be made that the understanding of this phrase becomes more difficult *because* it's exclusively found in the Book of Daniel. Let me explain why: Remember, the Book of Daniel was written during a time when the sanctuary in Jerusalem was desolate. The sanctuary was the instrument that facilitated the sacrificial system (Exodus 29:42); however, this instrument lay in ruins for most of Daniel's life. This fact makes it that much more difficult to determine how the Daily Sacrifice was relevant when, at that time, there was no sanctuary to facilitate a daily sacrifice. This is further complicated by the fact that Daniel mentions a 1290-day period in conjunction with the Daily Sacrifice (Daniel 12:11), but there are no significant events that took place 1290 days or years later.

Due to this uncertainty, I decided to dedicate

the next phase of my study to understanding how others interpreted the Daily Sacrifice. I didn't want to limit my research to Seventh-day Adventists; I wanted to know what other Christian denominations had to say about the Daily Sacrifice. If there were another viewpoint that made sense, I would not be opposed to embracing it as my own, but in order to find that one viewpoint, I had to study a variety of interpretations on this subject. Here is what I discovered.

Chapter 2

ANTIOCHUS EPIPHANES

In my studies, I discovered many Christians believe that the Daily Sacrifice refers to the literal animal sacrifices that occurred in Jerusalem. These Christians also believe that the *taking away of the Daily Sacrifice* referred to a historical event that resulted in the temporary termination of the Jewish sacrificial service. After the sanctuary was rebuilt, history records that a Syrian king temporarily put an end to these sacrifices. Here is what one commentary says:

> "We are informed by Josephus, by the author of the Maccabees, and others, that Antiochus's soldiers entered the temple and plundered it, and that afterward he ordered that the Jews should not be suffered to offer up the daily sacrifices, which, according to the law, they were accustomed to offer; that he compelled them also to omit their worship of the true God,

> and to pay divine honours to them whom he regarded as gods, and to make shrines in every city and village, and to build altars, and daily to sacrifice swine upon them: see Joseph. Antiq. lib. 12. cap. 5, sec. 4." *Commentary of the Old and New Testaments by Rev. Joseph Benson*

Antiochus IV Epiphanes - Altes Museum - Berlin - Germany 2017

According to Joseph Benson, Daniel's Daily Sacrifice referred to the literal sacrifices of the Jewish sanctuary. He and many others believe that a Syrian king named Antiochus Epiphanes was the individual Daniel prophesied would be responsible for taking away the sacrifices that had resumed years after Daniel's death. So who was Antiochus Epiphanes, and why did he take away the daily sacrifices? History says that in the 2nd century BC, the Palestine region was under Syrian rule. At that time, the King of Syria, Antiochus IV (also known as Antiochus Epiphanes), had replaced the Jewish high priest with an individual who made a large tribute to the Syrian king. This replacement of the High Priest resulted in a Jewish revolt. In 167 BC, Antiochus responded to that revolt by taking Jerusalem by storm, forbidding the worship of Yahweh, and banning all Jewish rites, including sacrificial offerings, for approximately three years.[2] This affliction is what many believe Daniel was referring to when he wrote, "*...and by him the daily sacrifice was taken away.*"

Since I initially believed the Daily Sacrifice referred to the Jewish temple sacrifices, I could see why so many Christians had logically drawn a connection between Daniel's Daily Sacrifice and the temple sacrifices in Jerusalem. I could also understand why many Christians believe Antiochus was the individual who took those sacrifices away. However, without getting into the minutiae of this belief system, I began to understand that accepting this viewpoint presented a number of issues.

1). Why would Daniel put so much emphasis on an obscure Syrian king for his role in prohibiting the Jewish sacrifices, when the Romans went beyond prohibition and destroyed the sanctuary and the city, which abolished the whole sacrificial system? I don't wish to minimize the atrocities that Antiochus

---

[2] Encyclopædia Britannica, s.v. "Antiochus IV Epiphanes," last modified November 13, 2019, https://www.britannica.com/biography/Antiochus-IV-Epiphanes

committed, but those atrocities pale in comparison to what the Romans did to the Jews.

2). Antiochus took away the Jewish sacrifices, but those sacrifices resumed approximately three years later. However, when the Romans took away the Jewish sacrifices in 70 AD, those sacrifices still have not resumed 1,950 years later. It doesn't make sense for Daniel to place this much significance on a three-year pause and essentially ignore a 2,000-year termination.

3). The Bible's description of the fourth kingdom does not match Antiochus. In Daniel 7:3, the prophet saw four beasts rise from the sea. These four beasts symbolized the same four kingdoms that the image in Daniel 2 represented: Babylon, Medo-Persia, Greece, and Rome.[3] According to Daniel 7:7-8, the Little Horn would rise out of this fourth kingdom. Notice how Daniel describes this ascension:

> "After this I saw in the night visions, and behold a fourth beast, dreadful and terrible, and strong exceedingly; and it had great iron teeth: it devoured and brake in pieces, and stamped the residue with the feet of it: and it was diverse from all the beasts that were before it; and it had

---

[3] SDA Bible Commentary Vol 4, p. 820-828

> ten horns. I considered the horns, and, behold, there came up among them another little horn, before whom there were three of the first horns plucked up by the roots: and, behold, in this horn were eyes like the eyes of man, and a mouth speaking great things." Daniel 7:7-8

Ladies and Gentlemen, if Antiochus were the Little Horn rising out of the fourth kingdom, that would make Syria the fourth kingdom as opposed to Rome. If we believe Syria was this fourth kingdom, we will have to ask ourselves—Was Syria more dreadful than Rome? Was Syria diverse from all the other nations? Did Syria ever devour the whole earth, and tread it down, and break it into pieces? We don't need to be historians to realize that Daniel's description of the fourth kingdom does not relate to the nation of Syria. However, if we look at the Roman Empire, it was diverse from the previous world powers because it was the first world empire to convert to Christianity. At the height of Rome's dominance, it ruled the known world, and the other nations were forced to submit to the will of the Eternal City. This dominance is why scripture declares Rome *devoured the whole earth, trod it down, and broke it into pieces.*

4). Antiochus Epiphanes was not greater than Alexander the Great. In Daniel 8, the prophet saw a goat with a great horn; this horn represented the kingdom of Greece. Notice how Daniel described this nation:

> "Therefore the he goat waxed **very great**: and when he was strong, the great horn was broken; and for it came up four notable ones toward the four winds of heaven." Daniel 8:8

Greece, under Alexander the Great was VERY GREAT. However, notice how Daniel described the Little Horn that came after the goat:

> "And out of one of them came forth a little horn, which waxed **EXCEEDING GREAT**, toward the south, and toward the east, and toward the pleasant land." Daniel 8:9

Did you catch that? Let me ask you a simple question—Is there any history book in the world that will tell you the Syrian King, Antiochus Epiphanes, was greater than Alexander the Great? Of course not. There is no metric in existence today that can make a case that Antiochus Epiphanes was EXCEEDING GREAT over Alexander of Greece. This idea would almost be laughable except for the fact that many Christians have embraced this belief, which makes this a sad reality. So even though Antiochus committed many terrible acts, including the temporary abolishment of the Jewish sacrifices, the historical context of his actions doesn't appear to match the prophetic context of Daniel's *taking away of the Daily Sacrifice.*

It was clear to me that the Daily Sacrifice was not referring to the Jewish sacrificial system, and it was also clear to me that the individual who took these sacrifices away was not Antiochus Epiphanes.

Chapter 3

THE CRUCIFIXION

Among the belief systems that attempt to define the Daily Sacrifice is the belief that the Daily Sacrifice represents the literal Jewish sacrificial system being taken away by the Crucifixion of Christ. Considering the attention Daniel gives to the Daily Sacrifice and its importance to our salvation, it is very plausible to believe the taking away of the Daily Sacrifice and the Crucifixion to be the same event.

As you know, one of my biggest gripes with the Antiochus theory is that he is just not relevant enough to match the attention given by Daniel to this event. However, who is more relevant than Christ? This becomes even more evident when we consider all scriptures lead back to Him. Remember, it was Jesus that said, "*Search the scriptures; for in them ye think ye have eternal life: and they are they which testify of me.*" John 5:29. Jesus clearly says the scriptures testify of Him of Him, so it is not beyond the pale to believe the scriptures regarding the Daily Sacrifice are directly testifying of Christ.

As I studied this prophetic theory, I discovered there are a few references where Daniel directly refers to the Crucifixion of Christ, but the problem was, these references to the Crucifixion were never associated with the Daily Sacrifice. Let me show you what I mean:

Daniel brings to light a prophecy that would last for 70 prophetic weeks or 490 literal years in the ninth chapter of his book. In simple terms, the 490-year prophecy refers to the length of time allotted to the Jewish nation to put away sin, accept the Messiah, and become the people of God that they were called to be. One of the benchmarks that would indicate they were close to the end of that allotted time was the Crucifixion of Christ. Daniel prophesied that Jesus would be killed three and a half prophetic days (or three and a half literal years) before the allotted time was over. Notice what Daniel says regarding this event:

> "And he shall confirm the covenant with many for one week: and in the midst of the week he shall cause the sacrifice and the oblation to cease..." Daniel 9:27[4]

---

[4] According to Ezekiel 4:6, prophecy often refers to years as days; hence the 70 weeks are 490 years.

Notice, Daniel mentions the sacrifice and the oblation ceasing but does not mention anything about the Daily Sacrifice. Let's look at another scriptural reference that appears to also point to the Crucifixion of Christ:

> "And with the arms of a flood shall they be overflown from before him, and shall be broken; yea, also the prince of the covenant." Daniel 11:22

This scripture also appears to refer to the Crucifixion. Only Christ can be the Prince of the Covenant, considering He was the One who confirmed the covenant in Daniel 9:27. This scripture speaks of being *broken*, which I believe alludes to the fact that Jesus Christ was killed by the Romans. Once again, we see that the Daily Sacrifice is not mentioned in conjunction with the Crucifixion of Christ. This omission is important as it opens the possibility that when Daniel referred to the Daily Sacrifice, he was not talking about the sacrificial system that ceased with the death of Christ.

Interestingly, Daniel 11 refers to the Daily Sacrifice, in verse 31:

> "And arms shall stand on his part, and they shall pollute the sanctuary of strength, and shall take away the

> daily sacrifice, and they shall place the abomination that maketh desolate."

This also begs us to answer the following question: If Daniel 11:22 is referring to the Crucifixion of Christ, then why does Daniel introduce the taking away of the Daily Sacrifice nine verses later? Daniel 11 is a chronologically written chapter. If the Crucifixion of Christ occurs in verse 22, and the Daily Sacrifice occurs in verse 31, then, chronologically, the Daily Sacrifice and the Crucifixion of Christ cannot be the same thing.

There are other red flags that indicate the Daily Sacrifice has nothing to do with the Crucifixion of Christ. Daniel 12:11 speaks about a 1290-day period occurring between the taking away of the Daily Sacrifice and the setting up of something called the Abomination of Desolation. Now, because the Abomination of Desolation is a separate subject, I will not delve into the details of its meaning. However, I will tell you that I believe the Abomination of Desolation refers to the work of Papal Rome. (Did I tell you that I also have a book called *The Clear and Present Truth of The Abomination of Desolation* that explains this in detail?).

Christ was crucified in 31 AD. However, 1290 days or 43 months later, nothing of significance happened that would be considered as the

Abomination of Desolation. It is true, Stephen was stoned in 34 AD, but the Abomination of Desolation never represented the stoning of anyone at any other point in scripture, and it was hard for me to believe that this particular stoning warranted a different interpretation. If we were to take the 1290 days as prophetic, that would turn the 1290-day prophecy into a 1290-year prophecy (See Ezekiel 4:6 for the day-for-a-year principle). However, due to a lack of any significant events, I think it's safe to say that the Abomination of Desolation did not occur in 1321 AD.

You may disagree; however, it was clear to me that there were just too many red flags that prohibited me from making a connection between the Crucifixion of Christ and the event known as the taking away of the Daily Sacrifice.

Chapter 4

A *Supplied* WORD

As I got deeper into studying the Daily Sacrifice, I was reminded that the King James translators often added words to verses to ensure the English translation was grammatically coherent. Today, these words are known as *supplied words*. The King James Bible italicizes these words making them easy to recognize. Even though the supplied words are not part of the original text, without them, the translation from Hebrew to English may be challenging to read.

For example, in Genesis 1:9, the Bible says:

> "And God said, Let the waters under the heaven be gathered together unto one place, and let the dry *land* appear: and it was so."

Since "land" is italicized, we understand that this word was added to ensure the text would properly flow in English. Without it, the text would read "...and let the dry appear." While it is still possible to determine the meaning of this text without the supplied word, I think it's safe to say, overall, the inclusion of supplied words adds a level of readability to a Book many deem hard to understand.

That being understood, we must also be mindful that even though the supplied words are generally considered helpful, they were added by men who were not under inspiration. Therefore, when deciphering the meaning of scripture, if there are italicized words within the text, make sure your interpretation of the text is not solely based on the supplied words. This may produce an incorrect interpretation of the text. The supplied words should *complement* the meaning of the text, not *determine* the meaning of the text. This is a crucial point, and I want you to understand it because what I'm about to show you is that some of us are allowing a supplied word to determine the meaning of the Daily Sacrifice!

You see, when I looked back at all the references Daniel made to the Daily Sacrifice, I realized that in every instance, the word "Sacrifice" was italicized! This means the translators added this word, not Daniel.

Now you are about to see, not only has "sacrifice" been erroneously added, but the addition of this word actually changed the meaning of the verse. I am not an English major, and grammar is not a strong suit of mine; however, I want you to understand the effects of adding the word Sacrifice to the Daily.

English sentences are made up of multiple parts. There is a noun, a pronoun, a verb, an adjective, an adverb, and so on. When we look at the word Daily and Sacrifice, we must understand that "Daily" acts as an adjective (a description) to the word "Sacrifice," which here is a noun (a thing).

Let's simplify this: imagine if I were to tell you that "I have a red car." Red (the adjective) describes what my car (the noun) looks like; however, the car is the central focus of the sentence. But what if you found out that *car* should not be part of the sentence? This changes the meaning of the whole sentence. Instead of me saying, "I have a red car," I would just say, "I have red." Initially, "red" was the adjective, but now it becomes the noun. I hope you understand my point here. What I'm trying to tell you is that the Daily is not the adjective; the Daily is the noun! By adding the word Sacrifice after the Daily, the translators have made Sacrifice the focal point of the sentence, which relegates the word Daily as merely a description of the Sacrifice. However, you should know that the Daily *is* the focal point of the verse, and Sacrifice does not belong in the text. If you can understand this point, then you should also know that this presents an obvious question: Why would the translators add the word Sacrifice to the Daily? I pondered this question for some time, but once I did a little research, the answer became obvious: The word Daily is translated from the Hebrew word *tâmîyd*. In the original language, *tâmîyd*, which means continual, is often associated with the continual burnt offerings. We see a clear example of this in Exodus 29:42:

> "*This shall be* a continual [*tâmîyd*] burnt offering throughout your generations at the door of the tabernacle of the congregation before the LORD: where I will meet you, to speak there unto thee."

Both continual and daily are translations of the Hebrew word *tâmîyd*. According to the Seventh-day Adventist Bible Commentary, *tâmîyd* is used frequently in connection with the ritual of the sanctuary.[5] This is compounded when we consider that three of the five scriptures that refer to the Daily also mention the sanctuary. So, if *tâmîyd* often refers to a component of the sanctuary service, and three of the fives scriptures that have *tâmîyd* also mention the word sanctuary, it is easy to see why the translators added the word Sacrifice to the scriptures that contained the word Daily. These translators appear to

---

[5] SDA Bible Commentary Vol 4, p. 842

have weighed the evidence and the context and added the word "sacrifice" in order to make the scriptures grammatically flow. The translators probably weren't able to make sense of how "a daily" could be taken away and therefore added sacrifice to the text believing they were making the verse more comprehensible. There's only one problem—the translators were wrong.

I have no doubt that most of the supplied words in the King James Bibles are beneficial to those of us who utilize it. However, adding Sacrifice to the text containing the Daily has completely changed the intended message that Daniel was trying to convey.

Ellen White, who is considered by many Seventh-day Adventists (SDA) as a source for Bible commentary, expresses this same sentiment in the below quotation:

> "Then I saw in relation to the 'Daily,' that the word 'sacrifice' was supplied by man's wisdom, and does not belong to the text."[6]

Understand, if we didn't know that Sacrifice was a supplied word, our attention would be focused on a sacrifice-related interpretation; however, it

[6] White, "A Sketch of the Christian Experience and Views of Ellen G. White," 61

should be clear to us now that Daniel is not referring to a sacrifice. Our focus now shifts from searching for a sacrifice to searching for the meaning of "the Daily"—or better translated as, "the Continual."

Chapter 5

Paganism

The Seventh-day Adventist Bible Commentary suggests that one of the more common views held by Seventh-day Adventists is the belief that the Daily represents Paganism. Regarding this belief, the Seventh-day Adventist Commentary on Daniel 8:11 states the following:

> "...the word for 'daily,' correctly meaning 'continual,' refers to the long continuance of Satan's opposition to the work of Christ through the medium of paganism; that the taking away of the daily and the setting up of 'the abomination that maketh desolate' represents papal Rome replacing pagan Rome, and that this event is the same as described in 2Thess 2:7 and Rev. *The Seventh Day Adventist Bible Commentary*, p. 843

The Seventh-day Adventist Bible Commentary correlates the Daily being replaced by the Abomination of Desolation, with Pagan Rome being succeeded by Papal (Catholic) Rome. In essence, Paganism, representing the Daily, was taken away and replaced by Catholicism, the Abomination of Desolation.

Uriah Smith, a Seventh-day Adventist pioneer, also held the belief that the Daily represented Paganism. In his book, *Daniel and the Revelation*, he states the following:

> "It was shown in comments on Daniel 8: 13, that 'sacrifice' is a word erroneously supplied. It should be 'desolation.' It seems clear therefore that the 'daily' desolation was paganism." *Daniel and the Revelation* p. 271

Uriah Smith and many Seventh-day Adventists today hold the belief that the Daily represents Paganism. However, I must admit to you that I never agreed with this view. While I can certainly understand why many SDA's have adopted this viewpoint, it was apparent to me that accepting this viewpoint presented a number of fundamental flaws. Let me show you what I mean. Daniel 8:12 says,

> "And an host was given *him* against

> the daily *sacrifice* by reason of transgression, and it cast down the truth to the ground; and it practised, and prospered."

If we accept the belief that the Daily represents Paganism, then the above scripture is telling us that transgression was how the Papacy came against Paganism and took it away. As Seventh-day Adventists, we know that Catholicism is essentially a repackaged version of Paganism. So how can one form of Paganism use transgression against another form of Paganism? It would be like Witchcraft using evil against Voodoo. I know this analogy may come across as very potent, but I want us to understand that Catholicism is Paganism disguised as Christianity. Notice how Ellen White conveys this same idea:

> "The nominal conversion of Constantine, in the early part of the fourth century, caused great rejoicing; and the world, cloaked with a form of righteousness, walked into the church. Now the work of corruption rapidly progressed. Paganism, while appearing to be vanquished, became the conqueror. Her spirit controlled the church. Her doctrines, ceremonies, and

> superstitions were incorporated into the faith and worship of the professed followers of Christ." *The Great Controversy* 1888 p. 50

Ellen White understood that even though Catholicism overtook Paganism, Paganism was still running the show. It doesn't make sense to use transgression against Paganism to set up Catholicism.

Let's look at another scripture that highlights the problems with accepting Paganism as the meaning of the Daily. Notice what Daniel 11:31 says:

> "And arms shall stand on his part, and they shall pollute the sanctuary of strength, and shall take away the daily *sacrifice*, and they shall place the abomination that maketh desolate."

Notice how the polluting of the sanctuary precedes the taking away of the Daily and placement of the Abomination of Desolation. The question is—Whose sanctuary is being polluted? Again, if Paganism is being replaced by the Papacy, then that would mean the sanctuary of Paganism was being polluted by Catholicism. In essence, we have one form of Paganism, being polluted by another form of Paganism, which almost comes across as if Paganism is a lesser evil than Catholicism. This makes little sense to me. If I were to take a full bottle of poison and pour some of its contents into a half bottle of apple juice—what do I have? I now have two bottles of poison. Will the apple juice mixed with poison be any worse than the straight poison? The apple juice poison-mix may deceive potential drinkers into consuming it by having the appearance of apple juice, but at the end of the day, the results of drinking straight poison are the same as drinking the mixed poison. Both liquids, whether straight or mixed, will result in death. It is in this aspect that I conclude Paganism is not a lesser evil than Catholicism. Catholicism may be dangerous because it appears as a Christian religion, but at the end of the day, it has the same effect as the apple juice with poison—it will destroy you.

Ladies and Gentlemen, I still have respect for many of my peers who support the idea of the Daily being a representation of Paganism; however, as for me, it was evident that the Daily meant something else.

Ellen White's View

Proponents of the belief that the Daily refers to Paganism have pointed to various quotes from Ellen White's writings as proof that she supported the Daily-is-Paganism viewpoint. However, before we look at any of her statements, we first need to establish the proper historical context of why this view is popular among Seventh-day Adventists.

In the mid-1800s, a Baptist minister named William Miller started a movement consisting of individuals who were earnestly anticipating the coming of Christ. These individuals, who were known as Millerites, believed the scriptures pointed to the Second Coming of Christ in the year 1843 AD. When this prophecy failed, they later predicted the Second Coming would take place in 1844.[7] This failure would later be known as the Great Disappointment.

Prior to this Great Disappointment, Millerite supporters Charles Fitch and Apollos Hale produced a prophecy chart. This chart was supposed to serve as a visual representation of the many prophetic symbols and dates brought to light by William Miller and the Millerite movement.[8] This

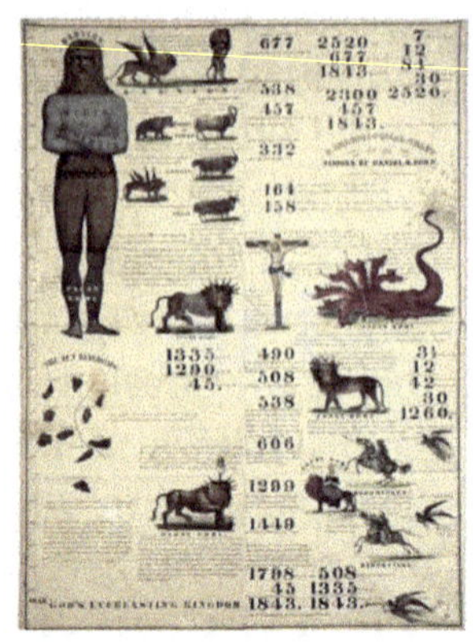

1843 Chart

---

[7] "Miller, William (1782-1849) ." American Eras. Encyclopedia.com. (August 11, 2020). https://www.encyclopedia.com/history/news-wires-white-papers-and-books/miller-william-1782-1849

[8] "Historical Data on "1843" Chart," Ministry Magazine Online, May 1942, https://www.ministrymagazine.org/archive/1942/05/historical-data-on-1843-chart

chart would later be known as the 1843 Chart.

This prophetic chart expressed William Miller's position regarding the Daily, which was a point of dispute. According to William Miller, the demise of Paganism is what he considered to be the taking away of the Daily.[9] However, the prevalent view of that era held that the Daily Sacrifice related to the Jewish sacrificial system. In response, William Miller's supporters brought to light that the word Sacrifice did not appear in the original Hebrew but was supplied by the translators of the Bible.[10]

Therefore, the 1843 chart inferred that the Daily represented the conversion of the Roman Empire which, by 508 AD, had fully converted from Paganism to Catholicism.

However, not everyone agreed with this view, and as a result, other competing theories began popping up. This would later result in Ellen White addressing the subject of the Daily Sacrifice with the following statement:

> "Then I saw in relation to the 'daily' (Daniel 8:12) that the word 'sacrifice'

---

[9] Miller, William. *Evidence from Scripture and History of the Second Coming of Christ about the Year 1843,* 95-96

[10] Litch, The Probability of the Second Coming, p. 34

> was supplied by man's wisdom, and does not belong to the text, and that the Lord gave the correct view of it to those who gave the judgment hour cry. When union existed, before 1844, nearly all were united on the correct view of the 'daily;' but in the confusion since 1844, other views have been embraced, and darkness and confusion have followed. Time has not been a test since 1844, and it will never again be a test." *Early Writings*, pp. 74-75

It almost appears that Ellen White *was* endorsing the Daily as expressed by the Millerites who were giving the judgment hour cry. If so, this would mean Ellen White also believed that the Daily represented Paganism.

However, before you run out and shout this from the rooftops, we must first understand that, while Ellen White is speaking about the Daily, the focal point of her statement is really about the word Sacrifice. If you look closely at her statement, she is trying to dispel the notion that the word Sacrifice should be included with the Daily. Now, why would she do that? Well, according to Julia Neuffer, a former editor at the Review and Herald Publishing Association, some Adventists had begun embracing the view that the Daily Sacrifice was "*a reference to the future restoration of Jewish Temple rites in Jerusalem.*"[11] If this is true, then it becomes clear why Ellen White made this statement about the Daily Sacrifice and why her initial focus centered on the fact that Sacrifice was a supplied word. Ellen White was trying to dispel the notion that the Daily Sacrifice referred to the Jewish sacrificial system. If believers in this new view could understand that "sacrifice" was erroneously added, maybe they would abandon the idea that the Daily Sacrifice referred to the restoration of the Jewish sacrificial system.

Ellen White then finishes her statement by saying, "*Time has not been a test since 1844, and it will never again be a test.*" Ellen White understood that if Adventists believed the Daily represented a future restoration of the temple in Jerusalem, then this would place the Daily sometime in the future. If the Daily was in the future, then this would compel Adventists to look for another time-based prophecy past 1844. Now it makes sense why Ellen White addressed this controversy with a declaration that the Millerites had the correct view of the Daily. If she could prove to Adventists that Sacrifice was a supplied word, then she could dispel the notion that Adventists should look for a future time-based prophecy based on

---

[11] Ellen White, *The Ellen G. White Letters and Manuscripts v1* (Silver Spring, Maryland: Ellen G. White Estate, 2016), p. 246

the restoration of the Jewish temple. Ellen White understood that if Adventists became preoccupied with this growing trend, the Church would lose focus on the Advent Movement.

Ellen White sensed the growing momentum behind this trend, which is why she supported the Millerite view that Sacrifice was a supplied word. Her focus was not on the Daily; her focus was on the Sacrifice.

This was not the only time Ellen White addressed this situation. Sometimes she addressed it more directly, as shown below:

> "Then I was pointed to some who are in the great error of believing that it is their duty to go to Old Jerusalem, and think they have a work to do there before the Lord comes. Such a view is calculated to take the mind and interest from the present work of the Lord, under the message of the third angel. For those who think that they are yet to go to Jerusalem, will have their minds there, and their means will be withheld from the cause of present truth, to get themselves and others to Jerusalem. I saw that such a mission would

> accomplish no real good." *A Sketch of the Christian Experience and Views of Ellen G. White*, p. 62.

Understand, Ellen White's initial statement about the Daily was not in support of the full Millerite view. Considering the context of her statements, it should be evident that the only part of the Millerite view Ellen White was expressing support for was the belief that Sacrifice was a supplied word.

You may be wondering—If Ellen White did not support William Miller's view, then what view did she support? The answer is none. Ellen White did not express support for the Millerite view on the Daily or any other view. She made it clear on multiple occasions that she had no light regarding the meaning of the Daily:

> "I now ask that my ministering brethren shall not make use of my writings in their arguments regarding this question; for **I have had no instruction on the point under discussion.**" *1Selected Messages* p. 164

> "**I have had no special light on the point presented for discussion** and I do not see the need of this

> discussion." *Manuscript Releases*, Vol. 12 p. 224

Ellen White was even interviewed regarding her statements on the Daily and the judgment hour cry. She was asked to clarify if she was endorsing Paganism as the meaning of the Daily. Elder Daniels, who was present during this interview, gave his account of the conversation, which is consistent with the above quotes. Here is what he said:

> "The only conclusion I could draw from her free explanation of the time and her silence as to the taking away of the "daily" and the casting down of the sanctuary was that the vision given her was regarding the time, and that she received no explanation as to the other parts of the prophecy." *Ellen G. White: The later Elmshaven Years*: 1905-1915 (Vol 6), p. 257

It was clear to me that Ellen White did not endorse Paganism as the meaning of the Daily. And while an argument can be made in favor of Paganism as the meaning of the Daily, these arguments weren't strong enough for me to embrace this view as gospel truth. I do have a lot of respect for William Miller and those who gave the judgment hour cry; however, it became clear that the Daily did not refer to Paganism.

Chapter 6

CHRIST'S HEAVENLY MINISTRATION

Another popular view of the Daily is that it represents the heavenly ministration of Jesus Christ. The subject of Jesus and the heavenly ministration is an in-depth subject; however, in simplified terms, this doctrine maintains the idea that there is a sanctuary in heaven. This heavenly sanctuary is where God the Father and God the Son are currently judging the saints.

We see various places in scripture that gives us clear evidence that there is a sanctuary in heaven. Notice what John the Revelator says:

"And the temple of God was opened

> **in heaven**, and there was seen in his temple the ark of his testament..." Revelation 11:19

We are also told that there is a judgment taking place. The Bible confirms this when it says:

> "Fear God, and give glory to him; for **the hour of his judgment is come**: and worship him that made heaven, and earth, and the sea, and the fountains of waters." Revelation 14:7

The judgment in heaven also means that Christ is interceding on our behalf. The Bible also confirms this fact when it says:

> "Wherefore he is able also to save them to the uttermost that come unto God by him, seeing **he ever liveth to make intercession for them**." Hebrews 7:25

As a Seventh-day Adventist, I place great importance on the heavenly ministration of Christ. This ministration is just as vital for our salvation as was His death on the cross. This is why I believe it is logical to embrace the heavenly ministration of Christ as the meaning behind the Daily. As a matter of fact, out of all the views I studied, I felt this one had the most logic to it. A scripture that is typically used to support this position is Daniel 11:31, which says:

> "And arms shall stand on his part, and they shall pollute the sanctuary of strength, and shall take away the daily *sacrifice*, and they shall place the abomination that maketh desolate."

Those who believe the Daily represents the heavenly ministration of Christ also believe the Abomination of Desolation refers to Roman Catholicism. In essence, this view declares that the taking away of the Daily and the placement of the Abomination that maketh desolate represents the Papacy taking away Christ's heavenly ministration and replacing it with the ministration of the Catholic priest.

I'm sure someone reading this book is asking the question—How in the world could anyone take away the heavenly ministration of Christ? Simple. When the Papacy came into power, it began securing authority that only Jesus could assume. For example, the Catholic Church claims to have the authority to forgive the sins of people.[12] This alone takes the focus

---

[12] Hanna, Edward, "Absolution" in The Catholic Encyclopedia. Vol. 1. New York: Robert Appleton Company, 1907. Retrieved August 19, 2020 from New Advent: http://www.newadvent.org/cathen/01061a.htm

from Christ and places that focus on a human.

Another example of how the Catholic church has taken away the heavenly ministration of Christ is the fact that the Catholic Church freely encourages its members to pray to dead saints.[13]

Now can you see why many consider the actions of the Catholic Church as the *taking away* of the Daily (assuming the Daily is the ministration of Christ)? This idea is further solidified when Paul tells us that the Antichrist sits in God's temple!

> "Let no man deceive you by any means: for *that* day *shall not come*, except there come a falling away first, and that man of sin be revealed, the son of perdition; Who opposeth and exalteth himself above all that is called God, or that is worshipped; so that he as God sitteth in the temple of God, shewing himself that he is God." 2Thessalonians 2:3-4

Even though I initially agreed with the rationale behind the Daily referring to the heavenly ministration of Christ, I realized that accepting this

---

[13] Kevin Knight, "The Summa Theologiæ of St. Thomas Aquinas" in The Catholic Encyclopedia Second and Revised Edition, 1920. Retrieved August 19, 2020 from New Advent: https://www.newadvent.org/summa/3083.htm#article4

position presented a problem: Daniel 8:13-14 reveals that the removal of the Daily was a temporary circumstance and that it would one day be restored. We know this because Daniel recorded a conversation between two angels that addressed the timeframe of the Daily being taken away:

> "Then I heard one saint speaking, and another saint said unto that certain *saint* which spake, **How long *shall be* the vision *concerning* the daily *sacrifice***, and the transgression of desolation, to give both the sanctuary and the host to be trodden under foot? And he said unto me, Unto two thousand and three hundred days; then shall the sanctuary be cleansed." Daniel 8:13-14

There are differing views on the 2300-day prophecy. Unfortunately, presenting an in-depth view on this subject would take away from this book's main focus. So instead, I will briefly summarize my position regarding this time-based prophecy:

The 2300-day prophecy refers to the heavenly sanctuary. According to Daniel, the sanctuary would be justified after 2300 days. Using the day-for-a-year principle (Number 14:34), we determine that this prophecy is actually 2300 *years*, starting in 457 BC (the command to restore and build Jerusalem) and ending in 1844 AD. If Christ's ministration in the heavenly sanctuary is the Daily, then this would mean that the Papacy's attack on Christ's ministration ended by 1844. The problem with this theory is that as late as 2013, there were an estimated 1.2 billion Catholics around the world.[14] Unfortunately, these Catholics are still praying to dead saints. Unfortunately, they are still attending confession and looking to their priests to forgive them of their sins. My point is, if the Daily is the heavenly ministration of Christ, how do we determine that the Daily has been restored after 1844? Whatever was taken away during the Dark Ages of Papal supremacy should be the same thing that was restored after 1844.

These questions were enough to give me pause in my assertion that the Daily represented the heavenly ministration of Christ. While I didn't completely rule this theory out, I decided to continue my studies, hoping God had another explanation that I overlooked. In the back of my mind, I knew that God had a plausible interpretation of the Daily, and I felt He would soon reveal it to me.

---

[14] "How many Roman Catholics are there in the world?" in BBC News, accessed August 20, 2020, https://www.bbc.com/news/world-21443313

Chapter 7

THE LAW

As I continued to ponder the subject of the Daily, I asked myself the question—Was there anything in history that was ever taken away and replaced by the Papacy? As I pondered this question, the thought occurred that the Papacy *did* take away the Sabbath. I quickly turned my Bible to Daniel 7:25, which tells us that this religious system would "think to change times and laws." The more I thought about this, the more sense it made. The Daily could actually be the Law of God! The Papacy freely admits that they changed the Sabbath from the seventh day of the week to the first day of the week.[15] In essence, the Papacy has taken away the Law of God. Remember, James 2:10 says, "*For whosoever shall keep the whole law, and yet offend in one point, he is guilty of all.*" By negating one commandment, the

[15] Stapleton, John. "The Ten Commandments." The Catholic Encyclopedia. Vol. 4. New York: Robert Appleton Company, 1908. 24 Jan. 2021 http://www.newadvent.org/cathen/04153a.htm.

Papacy negated the whole Law of God. If the Daily referred to the Law of God, then everything seemed to be pointing to the law as the meaning of the Daily.

However, it wasn't long after I embraced this idea that I realized I had to abandon it. Understand, Daniel 9 addresses the law of God in three different places. Let's review all three:

> "Neither have we obeyed the voice of the LORD our God, to walk in his **LAWS**, which he set before us by his servants the prophets." Daniel 9:10

> "Yea, all Israel have transgressed thy **LAW**, even by departing, that they might not obey thy voice; therefore the curse is poured upon us, and the oath that *is* written in the **LAW** of Moses the servant of God, because we have sinned against him." Daniel 9:11

> "As *it is* written in the **LAW** of Moses, all this evil is come upon us: yet made we not our prayer before the LORD our God, that we might turn from our iniquities, and understand thy truth." Daniel 9:13

As I read these verses, the thought occurred that each above scripture refers to the law by calling it "the law." I couldn't understand why Daniel would call God's commandments *the law* in chapter nine and refer to them as the Daily in all other places. If Daniel had not mentioned *the law* anywhere in his writings, then an argument could be made that the Daily referred to the law of God. However, the fact that Daniel calls God's requirements "the law" in chapter nine, led me to believe the Daily and the law were two separate subjects. This inexplicable inconsistency led me to abandon it as a potential viewpoint.

I knew God had the answer for me. All I had to do was trust in Him. I recalled that Matthew 21:22 tells us that if we ask, we shall receive, and that's exactly what I did. I continued to ask God for the truth of the Daily because I was not satisfied with the current interpretation. And just like that, He did!

Of course! After I exhausted almost every reasonable meaning of the Daily, there was only one other logical conclusion.

Chapter 8

THE DAILY IS...

It became increasingly clear what Daniel was trying to convey this whole time. However, in order for this to make sense, I need to recall the definition of the Daily for you:

> **The Daily** -" *Tâmîyd*," continuance (as indefinite extension); constant (or adverbially, constantly); elliptically the regular (daily) sacrifice:—alway(-s), continual (employment, -ly), daily, (n-)ever (-more), perpetual.[16]

According to Strong's Hebrew Lexicon, the Daily is defined as the CONTINUANCE. Let me ask you a question: Have you ever watched a television show

---

[16] "H8548 - tamiyd - Strong's Hebrew Lexicon (KJV)." Blue Letter Bible. Accessed 15 Aug, 2020. https://www.blueletterbible.org//lang/lexicon/lexicon.cfm?Strongs=H8548&t=KJV

that you were thoroughly enjoying, and then unexpectedly the show ended? The ending may feel unexpected because the story left too many unanswered questions. However, imagine before the credits begin, you see the words "To Be Continued" on the screen. These three words set a precedence that even though this particular show has ended, you now can expect a second phase of the show to be released in the future. You aren't told when this show will be released, and neither are you told the name this show will have. The only thing you know is that there will be a CONTINUANCE of the show. (I hope you are following me).

As God opened my eyes to the Book of Daniel, it dawned on me that Daniel understood something that we may not have realized he understood. Daniel, who was the recipient of the 70-weeks prophecy, knew that future Israel would fail! This is a critical point that needs to be clear. Remember, the 70-weeks prophecy was a length of time allotted to the Jews for them to get right with God. Notice what Daniel 9:24 says:

> "Seventy weeks are determined upon thy people and upon thy holy city, to finish the transgression, and to make an end of sins, and to make reconciliation for iniquity, and to bring in everlasting righteousness,

> and to seal up the vision and prophecy, and to anoint the most Holy."

We can see that Israel was allotted a certain amount of time to fulfill God's requirements. However, Daniel must have known that Israel would ultimately disobey God, for a few verses later, Gabriel said to Daniel,

> "...and the people of the prince that shall come shall destroy the city and the sanctuary; and the end thereof shall be with a flood, and unto the end of the war desolations are determined." Daniel 9:26

The destruction of Jerusalem and the sanctuary was a direct consequence of the Israelites not fulfilling their destiny. Jesus would later confirm the fate of Jerusalem when He said to them, "*Behold, your house is left unto you desolate.*" Matthew 23:38. Thus it was clear to Daniel that future Israel would eventually fail God. Notice how Ellen White explains this:

> "Thus Israel has been tested, tried, and cared for by the Lord. But they failed to fulfill His purposes for them. God longed to continue to bless His people, but selfishness

> took possession of the temple courts. **With prophetic eye Daniel looked down the ages and saw how the Jews would refuse to humble themselves.**" *Manuscript* 138, 1899

Since we've established that Daniel knew Israel would lose favor with God, I think it's important to understand how Israel currently relates to God's plans today. Understand, there is a doctrine floating around called Replacement Theology. This doctrine states that God established the Church to replace Israel as His chosen people after Israel failed. However, please understand this is a false teaching. The Bible clearly teaches that those who are Christs' are part of Israel:

> "And if ye be Christ's, then are ye Abraham's seed, and heirs according to the promise." Galatians 3:29.

Notice, the above scripture does not shun or shame the heritage of Abraham. On the contrary, Paul, writing to the Galatians, appears to confirm Abraham's descendants are still recognized by God. However, this recognition is no longer based on race or ethnicity. Notice how Paul expresses this same idea in the book of Romans:

> "But he *is* a Jew, which is one inwardly..." Romans 2:29

The inward Jew is anyone who accepts Jesus Christ into their heart as Lord and Savior, and through the power of the Holy Spirit, he or she becomes a Jew, or what is often called Spiritual Israel. There is no longer an exclusive club based on race or nationality. Even a person of Jewish heritage must also be graffed into Spiritual Israel. (see Romans 11:23).

Anyone who is tempted to think that the Church has replaced Israel needs to understand this one fact: Christianity is not a replacement of Israel; Christianity is a CONTINUATION of Israel!

Now it should become clear! Daniel understood there would be a second phase of Israel; however, he didn't know when nor what they would be called. He only knew they would succeed where Israel would fail. What Daniel called the Daily, or the Continual, is how he identified this remnant phase of God's people who would CONTINUE to serve God after national Israel's failure. Today, these remnant believers are known as Spiritual Israel, or more commonly—the Christian Church.

Notice how Ellen White conveys this very idea of the continuation of Israel through the church:

> "God's purposes have been moving steadily forward to their accomplishment. It was thus with Israel through the history of the

> divided monarchy; it is thus with spiritual Israel today." *From Splendor to Shadow*, p. 370
>
> "What God intended to do for the world through Israel, the chosen nation, He will finally accomplish through His church. He has entrusted "His vineyard to other vinedressers," who faithfully "render to Him the fruits in their seasons." These witnesses for God are the spiritual Israel, and God will fulfill to them all the covenant promises He made to His ancient people." *Royalty and Ruin* p. 250

In other words, Daniel looked at this "prophetic movie" called the Children of Israel, and he discovered that the movie abruptly ended. However, Daniel realized that even though national Israel failed, God would still have a people in the latter days to carry out His will. In essence, Daniel understood the "Israel movie" wasn't finished...it simply was "to be CONTINUED." Daniel revealed to us that one day the Continual would be taken away and replaced by another religious system known as the Abomination of Desolation.

This concept regarding the true Church being taken away and replaced by the Abomination of Desolation is also depicted in the Book of Revelation. John presents the true Church in the 12th chapter of Revelation as a pure woman. She was clothed with the sun (the New Covenant) and moon (the Old Covenant). And on her head, she had a crown of twelve stars (12 tribes of Israel and 12 Apostles of the church). She represents God's people, but more specially God's true Church of the New Testament. In other words, this pure woman represents the Daily.

The pure woman in Revelation 12

The harlot in Revelation 17

However, a few chapters later, we see a different woman. In

Revelation 17:3-5, John presents a filthy harlot. This begs the question—What happened to the pure woman? The answer is, she was taken away.

The first woman represents the Daily, and the second woman represents the Abomination of Desolation. The first woman was taken away in favor of the second woman. Daniel and John the Revelator may differ on how they refer to the ingredients of prophecy, but their recipes are the same: The Daily/Woman was taken away in favor of the Abomination of Desolation/ Mother of Harlots. However, before we close this book and anoint the Church-is-the-Daily theory as gospel truth, we must first test this idea as we did all the previous views.

The question needs to be asked: Did Daniel make any other reference to the Christian Church in his writings and label them anything other than the Daily? An argument can be made that Daniel did refer to the Christian church as Saints when he said,

> "And the kingdom and dominion, and the greatness of the kingdom under the whole heaven, shall be given to the people of the **SAINTS** of the most High, whose kingdom is an everlasting kingdom, and all dominions shall serve and obey him" Daniel 7:27.

The logical question here would be—Why would Daniel call the Christian church the Daily in chapter 8 but refer to them as saints in chapter 7? My answer is this: Daniel did indeed refer to God's people as "saints" in other places within his writings, but "saint" wasn't a title solely designated to the New Testament Church. The Scriptures record numerous occasions that Israelite men and women were also called saints (see 1 Samuel 2:9, Psalms 116:15, and Matthew 27:52). The usage of saints appears to be a general term for God's people regardless of the era. However, when Daniel says, "the Daily," it appears he is explicitly addressing God's people who succeeded the Children of Israel.

The word "Daily," is more than a generic term for believers. The Daily addresses the very fabric of the Church. This means the taking away of the Daily was more than persecution. The taking away of the Daily was a verbal, physical, and doctrinal attack against the Church to the point true Christianity nearly ceased to exist! Notice how Daniel describes this:

> "And he shall speak great words against the most High, and shall wear out the saints of the most High, and think to change times and laws: and they shall be given into his hand

> until a time and times and the dividing of time." Daniel 7:25

Understand, Daniel 7:25 provides us the method whereby the Daily was taken away. This Papal power spoke great words against the Most High by making numerous declarations that elevated the Pope in place of Christ.[17] This is how the Daily was verbally attacked. This attack resulted in Christians believing that the Bishop of Rome had the prerogatives of God Himself.

The wearing out of the Saints was the physical attack on the Church. Even recent Popes have attempted to apologize for the atrocities of the Dark Ages that took place under the Church's watch.[18]

Lastly, the thinking that times and laws had been changed was a spiritual attack against the Church's core beliefs. This attack resulted in the seventh-day Sabbath being discarded in favor of Sunday, and the endorsement of idol worship among other superstitious doctrines.

Ellen White also agrees that the Church was taken away when she says,

---

[17] Ellen White, *The Great Controversy* (Mountain View, CA: Pacific Press Publishing Association, 1911), p. 50

[18] Pullella, Philip. " Pope asks pardon from Waldensian Protestants for past persecution." *Reuters*, https://www.reuters.com/article/us-pope-turin-waldensians/pope-asks-pardon-from-waldensian-protestants-for-past-persecution-idUSKBN0P214F20150622. Accessed 29 August 2020.

> "The persecutions of Protestants by Romanism by which **the religion of Jesus Christ was almost annihilated**, will be more than rivalled when Protestantism and popery are combined." *Manuscript 30, 1889*

While I believe it's safe to say that both the Bible and Ellen White agree that the Church is the sequel to Israel, this still doesn't ultimately prove that the Daily is the Church.

We still must put the Daily-is-the-Church theory through the same tests that we put Antiochus Epiphanes and Paganism through. This view must be analyzed in the same fashion as the Crucifixion, the heavenly ministration of Christ, and the law of God. If the Church cannot pass the same tests we put the other theories through, then we must also reject this theory as we did all the other ones.

So let's continue (no pun intended) by going back to every scripture that contains the Daily Sacrifice, and substitute the word "Church" in its place and see if the church accurately fits into each scripture logically, chronologically, and historically:

> "Yea, he magnified *himself* even to the prince of the host, and by him the **CHURCH** was taken away, and

> the place of his sanctuary was cast down." Daniel 8:11

The Doctrine of Papal supremacy declares the Pope has supreme and universal power over the church.[19] This is one of the many ways the Papacy magnified itself as if it had the authority of Jesus Christ. History also confirms the sanctuary of the Christian church spiritually was cast down, and in some cases, the casting down was done literally. This means the Daily/Church theory matches the message of Daniel 8:11. Let's move on.

> "And an host was given *him* against the **CHURCH** by reason of transgression, and it cast down the truth to the ground; and it practised, and prospered." Daniel 8:12

Was Rome given a host or army of people that that was used against the church? Did Rome use transgression to achieve this? In case you didn't know, the answer is yes to both questions. The Papacy did not have its own army as other armies were used to do its bidding. As a matter of fact, King Clovis I of France was called the "Eldest Son of the Church."[20] This was

---

[19] Paragraph 882 of the Catechism of the Catholic Church (1997).

[20] "Remigius of Reims, St. ." New Catholic Encyclopedia. . Encyclopedia.com. (January 12, 2021). https://www.encyclopedia.com/religion/encyclopedias-almanacs-transcripts-and-maps/remigius-reims-st

the Papacy's host that was often used to do the bidding of the Church.

It is also true that Papal Rome asserted itself in place of Christ. It cast the truth down to the ground. It removed any remnants of the Sabbath. It made believers confess their sins to the priest and bow down to statues in prayer. Do you see how all of this is lining up? Now we can see how the Papacy used transgression to take away true Christianity.

Test two passed with flying colors. Let's move to test number three:

> "Then I heard one saint speaking, and another saint said unto that certain *saint* which spake, How long *shall* be the vision *concerning* **THE CHURCH**, and the transgression of desolation, to give both the sanctuary and the host to be trodden under foot?" Daniel 8:13

The question of "how long" reveals to us that the Papacy would only dominate the church for a certain time. The timeframe was 1260 years, which began with Papal supremacy in 538 AD and ended when Napoleon captured the Pope in 1798 AD. By 1844, the Papacy had lost its authority to speak great words against the Most High, Papal persecution had subsided, and Bible truth was being preached around the world. What was taken away had been restored. The question of "How long" had a viable answer, and the Daily/Church theory passed this test.

> "And arms shall stand on his part, and they shall pollute the sanctuary of strength, and shall take away **THE CHURCH**, and they shall place the abomination that maketh desolate." Daniel 11:31

Again, armies of Rome were used by the Papacy to pollute the Empire and take away true Christianity. Along with the removal of the church, we also see the placement of the Abomination of Desolation, which was the Roman Catholic Church. Chronologically, this makes sense. In order for the Papacy to assert its dominance, true Christianity had to be eliminated, which resulted in the true church fleeing to the mountains and caves. Revelation 12 refers to this persecution when it says, "*And when the dragon saw that he was cast unto the earth, he persecuted the woman which brought forth the man child.*" Revelation 12:13.

Let's now address our final test:

> "And from the time *that* **THE CHURCH** shall be taken away, and the abomination that maketh desolate set up, *there shall be* a

> thousand two hundred and ninety days." Daniel 12:11

In my book, *The Clear and Present Truth of the 2300, 1260, 1290, and 1335-day prophecies*, I confirm that historically, the events of the Church and the Papacy perfectly correlate with the 1290 days. I have no doubt in my mind that once you see how the 1290-day prophecy relates to the church, you will give this score a straight 5 out of 5!

Ladies, and Gentlemen, we no longer have a mystery on our hands. We no longer have to make excuses for the prophetically irrelevant Antiochus Epiphanes being the Daily. We no longer have to try to fit a square peg into a round hole by trying to make the Daily refer to the Crucifixion of Christ—an association never made by Daniel and chronologically inaccurate. We no longer need to step back into the 1800s and convince ourselves that Paganism is the Daily by trying to explain how one form of Paganism was used to transgress against another form of Paganism. We no longer have to accept the belief that the Daily was the ministration of Christ and ignore the fact that this ministration is still under attack by the millions of Catholics who look to their priests for the forgiveness of sins. And last but not least, we no longer have to make Daniel declare God's commandments as the law in one chapter and the Daily in another chapter. These theories are alleviated when we understand the Book of Daniel reveals that the Daily is the Church. The Church was taken away through persecution and doctrinal deceptions then replaced with a false religious system. However, after Daniel witnessed all of this, he saw the judgment taking place in Daniel 8:14. We must always keep in mind that God is still on the throne. He will set everything right in His time; all we must do is remain faithful to Him.

Ladies and Gentlemen, now do you see why I asked you to enter this journey with an open mind and a willing heart? Both are needed to accept this reality....the reality that says we are the Daily, we are the Continuance talked about in the Book of Daniel. This is the Clear and Present Truth of The Daily Sacrifice.

THE CLEAR AND PRESENT TRUTH OF THE

DAILY SACRIFICE

Test Your Knowledge

1. How many times does Daniel refer to the Daily Sacrifice in his writings? (p. 15)

   ____

2. Who was Antiochus Epiphanes? (pp. 20-21)

   ____

   ____

   ____

3. Give two reasons why Antiochus was not the individual who took away the Daily Sacrifice in the Book of Daniel. (pp. 21-25)

   ____

   ____

   ____

   ____

4. Provide a reason why the Daily Sacrifice does not refer to the Crucifixion of Christ. (pp. 27-31)

   ____

   ____

   ____

5. The King James translation has certain words that are italicized. What are those italicized words called, and why are they italicized? (pp. 33-34)

   ____

   ____

   ____

6. Explain how adding Sacrifice to the word Daily changes the construction of the sentence. (p. 35)

____

____

____

7. Why do some believe the Daily is Paganism? (p. 40)

____

____

____

8. What was Ellen White supporting when she endorsed the Millerite view of the Daily? (p. 49)

____

____

____

9. What problem is presented by accepting the heavenly ministration of Christ as the Daily? (pp. 57-58)

____

____

____

____

10. Why is it problematic to believe the Law of God is the Daily? (pp. 60-61)

____

____

____

11. According to the Hebrew Lexicon, what is the definition of the Daily? (p. 63)

____

____

12. The church has replaced Israel. True or False (p. 67)

13. Who or what does the Daily represent? (p. 67)

    ____

14. Daniel revealed the methods Catholicism used to take away the Daily. Name all three. (Daniel 7:25)

    ____

    ____

    ____

    ____

Test Your Knowledge - Answers

1. How many times does Daniel refer to the Daily Sacrifice in his writings? **Answer - Five times**

2. Who was Antiochus Epiphanes?
Answer - He was a Syrian King that stopped the Jewish sacrifices

3. Give two reasons why Antiochus was not the individual who took away the Daily Sacrifice in the Book of Daniel.
Answer - 1) The Little Horn was greater than the goat, Antiochus was not greater than Alexander the Great. 2) Syria was not the fourth kingdom listed by Daniel.

4. Provide a reason why the Daily Sacrifice does not refer to the Crucifixion of Christ.
Answer - Daniel speaks about the Crucifixion of Christ in Daniel 11; however, the Daily is referred to as a separate event.

5. The King James translation has certain words that are italicized. What are those italicized words called, and why are they italicized?
Answer - The italicized words in scripture are the supplied words. The translators added these words to make the English translation flow grammatically.

6. Explain how adding Sacrifice to the word Daily changes the construction of the sentence.

Answer - The Daily is the noun and is the focal point of the sentence. However, by place Sacrifice after the Daily, it turns the Daily into an adjective, and Sacrifice becomes the noun. Sacrifice becomes the focal point of the scripture.

7. Why do some believe the Daily is Paganism?
   Answer - Many believe Paganism is the Daily because the Daily was taken away and replaced by the Abomination of Desolation, and Paganism was taken away and replaced by Catholicism.

8. What was Ellen White supporting when she endorsed the Millerite view of the Daily?
   Answer - Ellen White was endorsing their view that the Sacrifice was a supplied word

9. What problem is presented by accepting the heavenly ministration of Christ as the Daily?
   Answer - If the Papacy's power to forgive sins is considered an attack on the heavenly ministration of Christ and the taking away of the Daily, then according to Daniel 8:13-14, that attack would have ended. However, millions of Catholics still look towards their priest for the forgiveness of sins.

10. Why is it problematic to believe the Law of God is the Daily?
    Answer - When Daniel speaks of the law in other places, he calls it *the law*. Therefore it is unlikely that the Daily and the Law are the same.

11. According to the Hebrew Lexicon, what is the definition of the Daily?
    Answer - The Continuance

12. The Church has replaced Israel True or False
    Answer - False

13. Who or what does the Daily represent?
    Answer - The Church

14. Daniel revealed the methods Catholicism used to take away the Daily. Name all three.
    a. The Papacy shall speak great words against the Most High with its declarations of supremacy.
    b. By persecuting the Saints and making the Church go into hiding.
    c. Deceiving the world into believing the Law of God has been changed.

www.ingramcontent.com/pod-product-compliance
Ingram Content Group UK Ltd.
Pitfield, Milton Keynes, MK11 3LW, UK
UKHW021826270726
14058UKWH00001B/3